A Family in Hawaii

This book takes you on a journey to the group
of islands in the Pacific Ocean called Hawaii.
You will fly to the bustling capital city of
Honolulu and then drive out along the coast to
the region where the Stagner family live. You
will discover what they do, what they like to eat
and what their hobbies and interests are.

A FAMILY IN
HAWAII

Jacobsen and Kristensen

The Bookwright Press
New York · 1986

Families Around the World

A Family in Australia
A Family in Central America
A Family in Colombia
A Family in China
A Family in France
A Family in Greenland
A Family in Hawaii
A Family in Holland
A Family in Hong Kong
A Family in Iceland

A Family in India
A Family in Ireland
A Family in Japan
A Family in Mexico
A Family in the Persian Gulf
A Family in Switzerland
A Family in Thailand
A Family in the U.S.S.R.
A Family in West Africa

First published in the
United States in 1986 by
The Bookwright Press
387 Park Avenue South
New York, NY 10016

First published in 1986 by
Wayland (Publishers) Limited
61 Western Road, Hove
East Sussex BN3 1JD, England
© Copyright 1986 Text and photographs
Peter Otto Jacobsen and Preben Sejer Kristensen
© Copyright 1986 English-language edition
Wayland (Publishers) Limited

Phototypeset by Kalligraphics Limited
Redhill, Surrey
Printed in Italy by G. Canale and C.S.p.A., Turin

ISBN 0–531–18084–0
Library of Congress Catalog Card Number: 85–73677

Contents

Flying to Hawaii

We leave San Francisco early in the morning, to fly west to the islands of Hawaii.

Hawaii is a group of volcanic islands in the Pacific Ocean, midway between the United States and Japan. There are eight main islands – Nihau, Kauai,

Hawaii – a group of exotic islands in the middle of the Pacific Ocean, discovered by Captain Cook.

Oahu, Molokai, Lanai, Kahoolawe, Maui and Hawaii – and 124 tiny ones. They cover a distance of 2,400 kilometers (1,500 miles) from west to east. The islands are volcanic mountains, which are almost completely submerged beneath the ocean. Although they lie in the area of the world where the climate is tropical, they have temperate weather.

The islands were first discovered by Captain James Cook in 1778. When he returned a year later, he was attacked and killed by natives.

We are flying 3,835 kilometers (2,397 miles) from the west coast of the United States, over the blue Pacific Ocean. Our destination is Honolulu, the capital of Hawaii, which is on Oahu Island. We will be landing at Honolulu International Airport, one of the two major airports in the country.

There are about 130 islands that make up Hawaii, stretching over 2,400 kilometers (1,500 miles) from west to east.

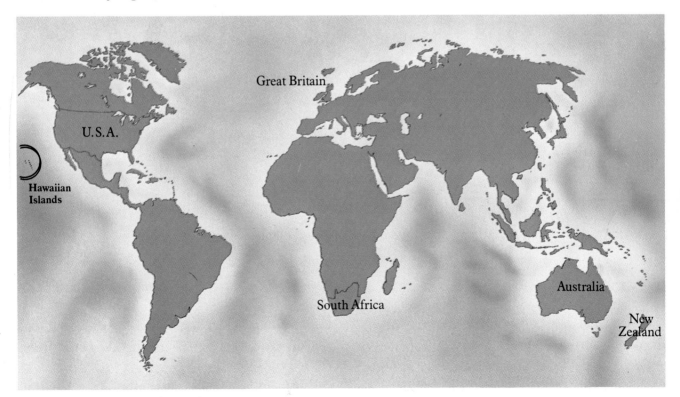

A day in Honolulu

Honolulu, the capital of Hawaii, is a modern city of skyscrapers.

We stay overnight in Honolulu, so that we have the chance to explore this capital city, before continuing our journey to meet the Stagner family.

Honolulu is a modern city, with soaring skyscrapers and broad boulevards, lined with coconut palms. It is situated on the southern side of Oahu Island, with the Koolau Mountains rising up behind. As the capital of Hawaii, Honolulu contains the Royal Palace. It is called the Iolani Palace and was built by King Kalahaua. Near the Palace stands Kawaiahao Church, which is where the kings of Hawaii were crowned in the days before the arrival of Europeans and Americans, about 100 years ago.

There are very few houses in Honolulu, only skyscrapers, which are mostly hotels. The streets are busy, packed with Japanese and American people. Most Hawaiians can't afford to live here, because the tourist industry has caused the price of property in the city to increase dramatically.

A customer stands in one of the many Chinese shops in Honolulu, which is packed with goods from the Far East.

We continue our exploration through Honolulu's Chinatown, an area of narrow, dimly lit streets, packed with stores selling all kinds of Chinese goods. There are restaurants and markets, too. Thousands of settlers came here from the countries of the Pacific, including China, bringing with them their native customs, languages and religions. This mixture of Pacific peoples with Asians and also with Westerners has existed in Hawaii for a

Honolulu's skyscrapers are built right down to the water's edge.

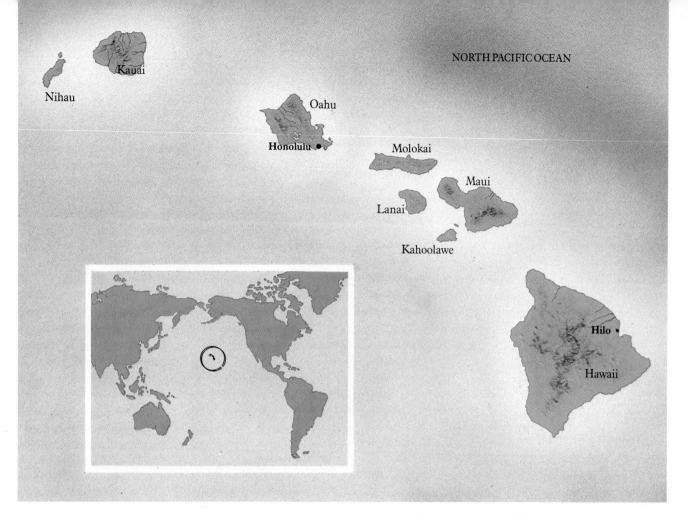

NORTH PACIFIC OCEAN

Nihau

Kauai

Oahu

Honolulu •

Molokai

Lanai

Maui

Kahoolawe

Hilo •

Hawaii

There are eight main islands in Hawaii. The capital, Honolulu, is on Oahu Island.

very long time.

We return to our air-conditioned skyscraper hotel to pick up our luggage and the car we have hired for the trip. It is essential to have a car on the islands of Hawaii. On Oahu there is a bus service, but on the other islands there is no public transportation. We drive on the freeway out of Honolulu, and head along the coast. The Stagners' home is 50 kilometers (31 miles) away.

We meet the Stagner family

Ishmael has fun taking Kekoa and Kauikeolani for a ride on his moped.

We leave the bustling, tourist capital behind and find ourselves driving through the beautiful countryside, with its lush foliage and waving palm trees on the sandy shores of the Pacific.

The Stagner family is waiting for us outside their home when we arrive.

Ishmael Stagner shakes us warmly by the hand and introduces us to his family – Carmen Rosita, his wife, and their five children. There are four boys – Kealoha

Carmen Rosita helps Makana to braid her hair.

who is 12, Kealii who is 14, Kekoa who is 5 and Kauikeolani who is just 3. Makana is the only girl, and she is 8 years old. All the children have both American and Hawaiian names but they have Hawaiian nicknames for everyday use.

Like most families in this area, the Stagners are Mormons. The Mormons are a religious group, which bases its beliefs on the teaching of the Prophet Mormon, in the *Book of Mormon*.

Ishmael built the family house himself. It is in a housing development where there are 600 other residents, of which 400 are children. Consequently, there are lots of facilities for children, including a playground with a basketball court and a soccer field. Both these sports are very popular in Hawaii.

Kealoha is 12 years old and goes to the local school. When he is 18 he hopes to go to college.

On the coast near the Stagners' home lots of people go windsurfing. It is a very popular sport in Hawaii.

15

Ishmael Stagner

Ishmael Stagner is 42 years old. He is a university lecturer. He teaches at the Mormon University.

"I usually teach about fifteen hours every week," he tells us. "The preparation for my teaching takes about forty hours each week. My work also involves advising students about their work, what courses they should take and any other problems they might have."

Ishmael feels guilty because his work takes up so much of his time, and he has less time to spend with his family.

"On the other hand," he adds, "I have to be able to pay the bills, and it's expensive living here in Hawaii."

Ishmael believes that the family comes first.

We ask him what he teaches at the university. "Some of the most interesting work I do is lecturing other teachers on how to teach the handicapped. I also teach Psychology and English."

Ishmael teaches at the Mormon university.

Apart from building and improving his house, Ishmael is interested in music and playing soccer.

17

Carmen Rosita Stagner

Carmen Rosita used to be a professional hula dancer, but now she has a big family to look after.

Carmen Rosita is 37 years old. She is now a full-time housewife, although she used to be a professional hula dancer. Like her husband, Ishmael, she was born and brought up in Hawaii, and she is also a Mormon.

"I was converted when I was 18 and just beginning my university course," she tells us. "I saw how happy my fellow students were and I wanted to share in it. Before then I was a Roman Catholic."

We ask her about hula dancing.

"I love to dance, and I have danced the hula since the age of five. I have had eight different instructors and took lessons for thirty years," she says. "The lessons begin at 5:30 a.m. and last for two hours, twice a week. But you have to train for four hours every day as well."

Carmen Rosita likes cooking, and sewing for the children, as well as making ceramics and candles. She also plays the piano and is learning to paint in oils.

We ask her how she met Ishmael. She grins at us.

"The first time I saw Ishmael was at the university when I was 20 years old.

Carmen Rosita makes candles and ceramics in her spare time. She is also learning to paint in oils.

It wasn't love at first sight. In fact, I didn't think much of him at all. But he was so persistent that I began to think that there must be something more to him. The next year we were married!"

Hawaiian customs

Both Ishmael and Carmen Rosita are enthusiastic about preserving Hawaiian culture.

"There were 200,000 Hawaiian people just 100 years ago. Today there are only 2,000, and so we are eager to preserve the old Hawaiian customs," Ishmael says.

Carmen Rosita tells us more about hula dancing. "There's no written language on Hawaii, so the hula dance is very important. Through the dance we express atmosphere and feeling. We can retell history and pass on myths and legends to people. That's why I like to dance, and in that way give expression to my race and its culture." The garlands of flowers, or *lei*, which are worn by the dancers, are still made by hand. The skirts they wear are handmade, too, from either bast or palm leaves.

"There is an Hawaiian tradition called *calabash*," Ishmael continues. "A *calabash* is a stranger who moves in with a family, where he can live freely for as long

Carmen Rosita has danced the hula since she was 5 years old.

20

as he likes. While he is there he is considered to be part of the family."

"*Hanai* is another Hawaiian tradition. It is an expression of Hawaiian hospitality. If a stranger asks if he can borrow your car, you tell him that whatever is yours is his too. If somebody is referred to as a *Hanai*, it means that they have been adopted and so have the right of inheritance," Ishmael concludes.

These hula dancers wear grass skirts and garlands of flowers, which are part of a very old Hawaiian tradition.

Family life

The family are hoping to go to the movies, but they cannot decide what film they should see.

The Stagner family are all Mormons and, as Ishmael tells us. "It is more a way of life than a religion."

He goes on, "Mormons attach great importance to the strength of the family. They do a lot to encourage fellowship in the family."

Carmen Rosita explains, "The family meets at least once a week to talk things over and to spend some time together. We make long and short term plans and then write our decisions up on the blackboard. We talk about anything that any member of the family brings up."

"We also take turns in deciding what we shall all do together on that day," says Kealii. "Sometimes we go cycling or bowling. We even bake bread together or go for a picnic. The main aim is to do something we all enjoy."

Every Sunday the whole family goes to Sunday school for three hours. They go to different classes and learn about different aspects of their religion and their family life. They also learn how to improve their skills.

Kekoa, who is 5 years old, likes to play soccer. There are lots of children for him to play with who live nearby.

23

Kealii, who is 14 years old, and his two brothers are helping in the garden.

24

"A good marriage means that each partner gives everything in order to make the other partner happy. A good husband should take care of his wife and children," Carmen Rosita explains. "His family is more important than his career. A good wife should care for both her husband and her children, equally."

Kealii and Kealoha are both Boy Scouts. They do plenty of work for the local community.

"We clean up the churchyard each week, and if there is anything one of the residents in the village needs doing, we help out," Kealoha says.

They also enjoy playing soccer and baseball. Sometimes they go swimming and fishing.

Makana, their sister, likes designing clothes. She has already won a competition. There were 6,000 entries for the competition to design a school uniform, and she won.

"I dance the hula, too," she tells us, "as my mother used to."

Makana is good at designing clothes. She has won first prize for designing a school uniform.

Mealtime

Carmen Rosita and Ishmael invite us to stay and eat some typical Hawaiian food with them. We are very happy to accept.

Carmen Rosita is preparing the family's favorite meal, which is *lomi* trout and *lau lau*.

"To make the *lomi* trout, you need filleted trout," she tells us. "You break up the raw fish with your fingers, and then mix it together with some onion and tomatoes, which have been finely chopped. You put it in a bowl and then serve it on a bed of crushed ice."

Lau lau is a mixture of pork, halibut and *taro* leaves (which taste something like spinach). The mixture is seasoned and then wrapped, in small amounts, in *ti* leaves (a type of palm leaf). These individual portions are then steamed for six hours. It's delicious.

After we finish eating we ask Ishmael and Carmen Rosita how they see the future.

"Our future is closely linked with our children," Carmen Rosita says. "We hope that the way we bring them up will give them a sense of their value."

Carmen Rosita has a modern kitchen with all the latest equipment.

Lomi *trout and* lau lau – *the Stagners' favorite dish.*

"We think it important that the two boys have a university education and we hope that they will serve as missionaries for 2½ years," Ishmael adds. "We hope that Makana will marry and have a family. It is more important that a girl do this, rather than becoming a missionary or having a university education."

"Our dream is to see our children married in the temple. But it is only the really good Mormons who get permission to do that. It is considered to be a great honor," Carmen Rosita concludes.

After we finish talking we have to leave the Stagner family and make our way back to Honolulu. Just as we are thanking them for the interesting and enjoyable day we spent with them, Carmen Rosita surprises us by giving us a garland of flowers each.

"We hope that these will remind you of your visit to the beautiful islands of Hawaii," she says smiling.

Left: *Carmen Rosita hopes the boys will go to college and then become Mormon missionaries.*

Right: *Carmen Rosita and Ishmael would like Makana to marry and bring up a family.*

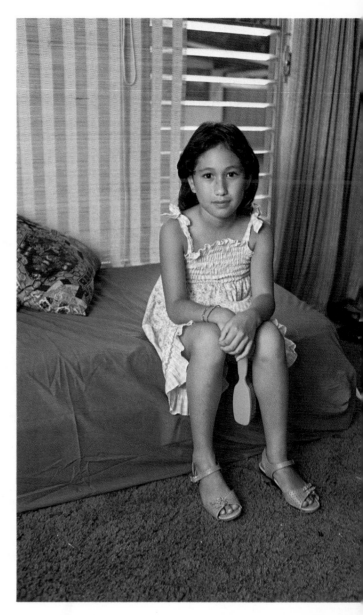

Facts about Hawaii

Size: The total land area is 16,641 sq. km. (6,425 sq. mi.).

Capital city: Honolulu, which is situated on Oahu Island.

Language: English. There are many immigrants, including Japanese, Chinese and Filippino, who speak their native languages.

Money: U.S. dollars.

Religion: There is a mixture of religions owing to the numbers of immigrants from China, Japan, the Philippines, Europe and America.

Climate: Hawaii has a temperate climate. The average temperature in Honolulu at the coolest time of the year is 22.2°C (71.9°F) and 25.8°C (78.4°F) at the hottest time of the year. The mountainous areas are much cooler. There are also big contrasts in the amount of annual rainfall across the country.

Government: In 1959 Hawaii became the 50th state. It is governed by a state constitution. A governor and lieutenant governor are elected for periods of 4 years. There is a Senate and a House of Representatives, which are also elected every 4 years.

Education: There are private and public schools for children up to college level. Then they can go to the University of Hawaii. There are five smaller private colleges of higher education and there are also private business, technical and specialized schools.

Agriculture: Despite the huge tourist industry, agriculture is still the backbone of the economy. Sugarcane and pineapples are the main crops. Hawaii produces 40 percent of the world's pineapple juice. There is also livestock, poultry and dairy farming.

Fishing: There is some commercial fishing, 50 percent of which is tuna fishing.

Industry: There is an oil refinery producing a variety of petroleum products, a steel mill, two cement plants and 80 clothing manufacturers, which are mostly in Honolulu.

Glossary

Bast The inner bark of a tree.

Boulevard A broad road bordered by trees.

Ceramics Objects that are made of clay.

Destination The place at the end of a journey.

Filleted fish A fish that has had its bones removed.

Foliage The leaves of trees or bushes.

Freeway A wide, fast road.

Garland A circle of flowers, woven together.

Inheritance The right to receive a person's money and property after he or she dies.

Missionary A person who is sent to other countries to spread a religion.

Natives People who belong to a particular country because they were born there.

Skyscraper An extremely tall building.

Volcanic Produced by, or relating to, an active volcano.

Index

Picture acknowledgments

All the illustrations in this book were supplied by the authors, with the exception of the following:
Camerapix Hutchison 6, 10, 15; Bruce Coleman/Werner Stoy 8, Bruce Coleman/Nicholas Devore
9; The maps on pages 7 and 11 were drawn by Bill Donohoe.